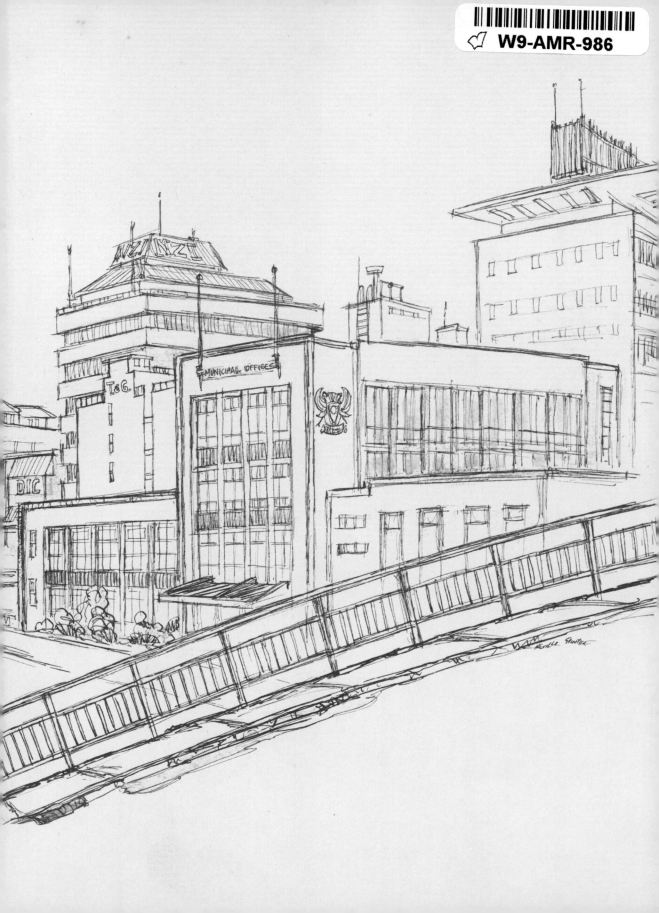

HAMILTON
and the Waikato

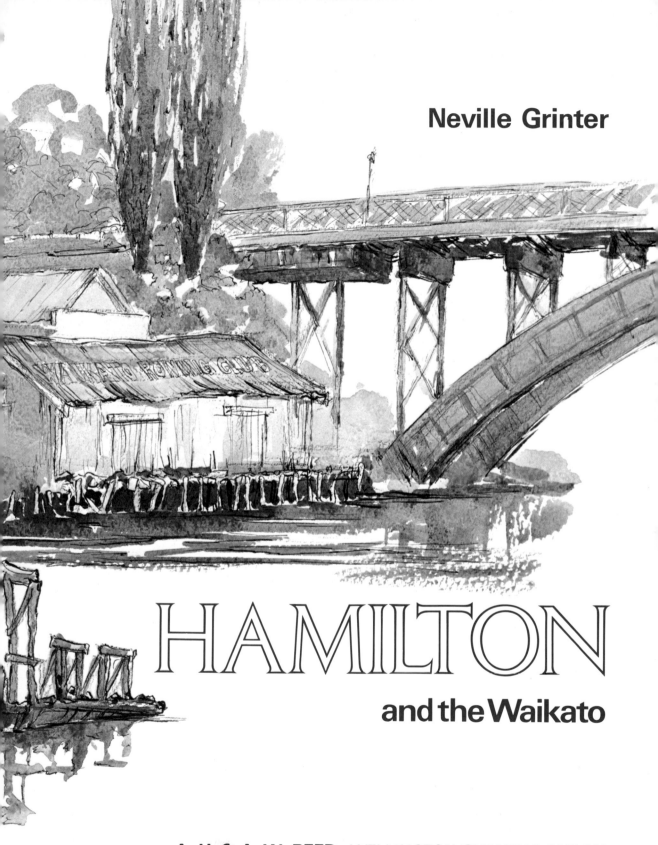

Neville Grinter

HAMILTON
and the Waikato

A. H. & A. W. REED : WELLINGTON/SYDNEY/LONDON

First published 1976

A.H. & A.W. REED LTD

182 Wakefield Street, Wellington
53 Myoora Road, Terrey Hills, Sydney 2084
11 Southampton Row, London WC1B 5HA
also
16 Beresford Street, Auckland
165 Cashel Street, Christchurch

ISBN 589 00971 0

Typeset on IBM Composer by A.H. & A.W. Reed Ltd, Wellington
Printed by Kyodo Printing Co. Ltd, Tokyo, Japan

FOREWORD

Mr Grinter has lived in Hamilton virtually all his life and is well acquainted with the changes which have taken place in the city and the neighbouring district in the past 40 years.

His selected paintings provide glimpses of the past as well as indications of the modern city of Hamilton which is now in the making. They provide a sensitive commentary upon what has gone before and upon what is now happening, both to Hamilton and to the district, with which the city retains continuing close association.

I am sure his work will be of interest to all who have past or present association with Hamilton and the Waikato district.

M.J. MINOGUE
Member of Parliament for
Hamilton West and former
Mayor of Hamilton

HAMILTON

Looking at Garden Place today encircled by towers of modern concrete buildings, it is hard to imagine the way it was when it was first named. Then it was a hill covering an area of a little over a hectare (two and three-quarter acres), rising 15 metres (50 feet) above Victoria Street to some large Norfolk Pines.

"The Hill" was a favourite meeting place with its ponga houses and rose-lined walkways. It was moved in 1939 by my father, who was contracted to do the job.

After a history of air-raid shelters and parking meters, the area was closed to vehicle traffic and developed into beautiful gardens, lawn and fountains. Sketching scenes to the soothing sound of the fountains, I found it easy to be lulled into lingering here longer than I had intended.

Old Garden Place, 1939

Garden Place

Hamilton's Victoria Street was reputedly called the "golden mile" for its flourishing businesses. But old-timers will tell you it's because of the quartz rock that was brought from the Karangahake Gorge near Waihi and used in places as foundations for the main street.

For many years the street was divided by a railway line in the centre of town; several times a day all traffic came to a halt as trains steamed their way through town and people late for an appointment fumed and steamed along with the train while they waited.

The lowering of the railway line in 1964 made it possible to cope with the modern flow of traffic.

Later years have seen the steady growth of multi-storeyed buildings, dramatically changing Hamilton's skyline. The modern university complex at Hillcrest and the park setting of the Founders Theatre blend beautifully with the residential setting. To the west of Hamilton stands the Mormon College, its impressive gleaming white church tower reaching skywards from the green rolling hills.

Mormon Temple

Opposite page:
Tudor Arcade

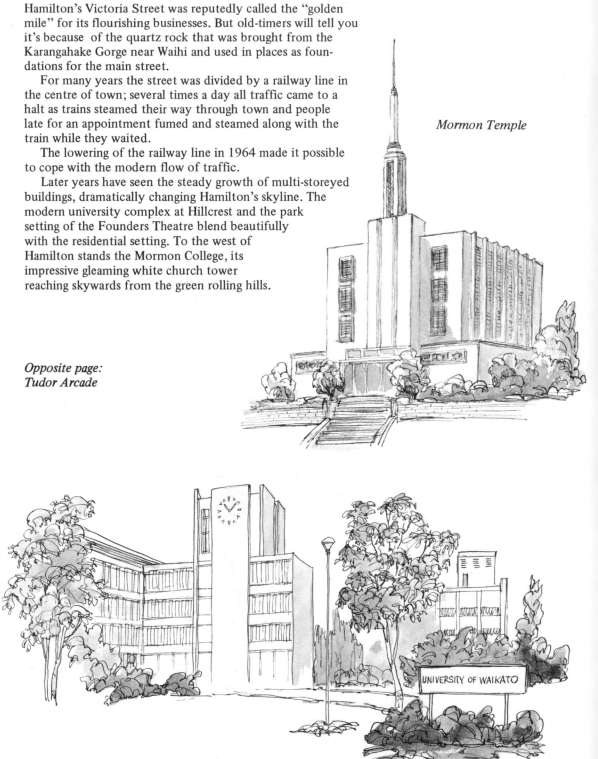

UNIVERSITY OF WAIKATO

Yachts on Lake Rotorua

Just a short walk from the main street I propped myself up under a nikau palm at Hamilton's Lake Rotorua and wondered how you describe peace. I have painted the Hamilton lake many times in its different moods, never failing to notice the relaxing effect that nearby water seems to have on people.

Power boats are prohibited here; the yachts seem to revel in their freedom, slipping quietly by as their colourful sails father the breeze, fitting into but not disturbing their environment. Nestled quietly in a setting of gum and acacia trees across the lake is the yacht club — today a blaze of colour as members prepare for a day's sport.

From the swings and slides drift the sounds of children at play. Ducks and swans gather around, eyeing my paint box over for something edible. It is good just to sit awhile.

Lake Rotorua

Parana Park

Frankton Saleyards

54-37

Tuesday at Hamilton has always been "Cockys' Day". There were even the days when the drovers used to drive their stock over the main Fairfield Bridge to the sale-yards at Frankton. This does not happen today. Modern memories of scenes such as this are very clear — as a boy I watched from our home by the bridge as the drovers struggled to get the leading cattle across while trying to stop the rest of the stock from doing too much damage to nearby gardens. At the Frankton saleyards the main change over the years has been in the quality and quantity of the cars parked outside. Little else seems to have changed.

Cattle on Fairfield Bridge, early 1950s

Old Frankton Station, early morning

Many people will remember staggering along the walkway of the Frankton railway over-bridge at 4 a.m. with too many suitcases. And that 10-hour trip from Wellington to Frankton Station on the night train. Somewhere up ahead in the darkness the smokey old "K" class engine clattered through the night as you tried to sleep propped up in your seat, wrestling with a railway pillow — which finished up on the floor anyhow. You'll also remember the taste of coal smoke washed down with tea provided in sturdy railway cups at endless stops on the way before you finally arrived at the old familiar station. The powerful railway shunting lights muted by damp early morning fog cast an unreal yellow glow across the scene as you looked out from the over-bridge at the sleeping city.

The station was opened in 1877 — during Queen Victoria's reign. The junction has done great service in New Zealand's transport system, but now this "oldy" has seen its last train. The new modern station further south has taken over, and demolition of the old station and its picturesque overbridge walkway has left only dust and memories.

"Breton", a now deserted homestead at Hillcrest, is one of the few visual reminders of a bygone era. It was built around 1870, a time when the pace of life was more leisurely.

Kings Chambers, another "oldy", was originally a picture theatre. Its high ceilings and archway entrance reveal its history. As a young girl my mother played the piano accompaniment to silent movies shown here.

THE OLD HOUSE

The loving and the laughter,
    The sadness and tears;
It has witnessed all these human things
    With the passing of the years.
Now all alone on the stage of life,
    Where the players come and go,
A worn out prop from another scene
    That no one wants to know.

The rolling land where the old house stands
    Was once man's greatest treasure.
There were trees and grass and the cattle grazed;
    Man moved about in leisure.
Now urban sprawl has devoured it all
    With the tide of man's endeavour.
The house, the land and a way of life
    Have been swept aside forever.

"Breton", Hillcrest

Kings Chambers

17

"Greenslade"

Old Frankton
stationmaster's house

Hamilton is of course an inland city, and is therefore lucky indeed to be blessed with the Waikato River. Its banks lined with graceful willows and birch trees, this beautiful river begins at the snow-clear waters of Lake Taupo and meanders peacefully through the lush, fertile Waikato farmlands.

When I was a boy the "big deal" was to swim across the Waikato River and back. On a sweltering Hamilton summer's day many pleasant hours were spent swinging from ropes on trees and drifting lazily down with the current. Boys haven't changed much, but unfortunately the river has. It is sad that in common with waterways in other places "progress" has brought pollution, denying the simple pleasures that we once enjoyed.

Hamilton has a fine new Olympic swimming pool under way, but meanwhile there are still the Municipal Baths (or the "Munis" as Hamiltonians know them) with their tangle of bikes scattered about outside and sounds of joyous fun from within.

The grasslands of the Waikato are among the richest dairy farming country in the world. As they roll gently across the landscape the paddocks are divided by fences and hedges into a colourful patchwork pattern, stretching away to a typical backdrop of distant blue hills. It is to the pastoral wealth of farmland such as this that Hamilton owes its growth and prosperity.

Sounds of a cowshed coming to life drift across the farm as the cows file into the yard. A radio blares against the background throb of milking machine pumps and the clatter of milk buckets on the concrete. This is a scene repeated daily in the lifetime of old cowsheds like this one; they have formed the backbone of the Waikato farming economy. Pensioned off in favour of a new "herring bone" shed, the old one is now used only to shelter farm equipment beneath its sagging tiled roof — a legacy of the war years when iron was not available.

Waikato dairy country

CAMBRIDGE

We all regard Cambridge, just 22 kilometres (14 miles) south of Hamilton, as a "typical English town". The old master John Constable would have been in his element here among the gardens and lake, the picturesque chiming clock tower and the stately old churches, all nestling in a setting of beautiful oak trees.

This is artist country, no doubt about it, but finding a scene typical of Cambridge proved more difficult than I had expected. This lively little town has a quiet overall charm hard to capture in a mere painting.

There is a quiet peace here that is very appealing to me. Even though the busy main highway runs right through the town, Cambridge has still retained its leisurely charm. I have always been amazed at the casual ways of the local motorists and pedestrians. There's none of that crazy big city rush and panic for them; they just stop the car (anywhere) and go walkabout. Nobody seems to hurry. It would be very easy to get used to.

Anglican church, Cambridge

Cambridge

24

NGARUAWAHIA

Ngaruawahia is synonymous with the Maori King Movement. Here is the official seat of the reigning Maori monarch at the Turangawaewae Pa, "a place to stand". This was a prophecy made by the second king, Tawhiao, during the Waikato wars in the 1860s.

It was here at Ngaruawahia, the place for "breaking open the food pits" nestled at the foot-hills of the Hakarimata Ranges,that the famous chief Potatau Te Wherowhero was recognised in June 1858 as the first Maori King and "matua" (father), to head the moves for Maori national unity and prevention of land sales.

In early European days Ngaruawahia threatened to rival Hamilton as the main settlement of the Waikato (the early settlers called it Newcastle, a reference to coal deposits nearby). But with the development of the railway link with Auckland, the importance of river transport declined and with it Ngaruawahia's chances of becoming a major city. Coal mining has now declined. With a present population of around 4,000 Ngaruawahia remains an important farming centre.

"Axemen stand to your blocks." The words from a public address system blare out across the sports park on the river bank where the Waipa joins the Waikato River at Ngaruawahia. Razor-sharp axes swing and huge chips fly as the line of powerfully built axemen carve through their logs with incredible speed and accuracy. In a friendly relaxed atmosphere at the local axemen's carnival, spectators lounge on the grass, sit on boxes or stand on the old truck, urging on their favourite. Children wander about with lemonade bottles and chunks of watermelon.

Ngaruawahia: axemen's carnival

TE AWAMUTU

Te Awamutu is widely known for its racing stables; some of the country's leading racehorses are trained here. Starting their day before daybreak, the jockeys and horses made an interesting study for painting in the early morning fog.

Te Awamutu is also the venue for an annual rose festival, a time when arts and crafts of all descriptions — as well as a wonderful variety of flowers — are on display in shops and around the streets. The town's carefully tended rose gardens make a beautiful showing when in bloom, giving meaning to the adopted name of "Rose Town".

Near Te Awamutu are the remains of Orakau Pa, the scene of the last great battle of the Waikato Wars. Hopelessly out-numbered, the famed Maori chief Rewi Maniapoto made his last stand here.

An early pioneer named Taylor owned literally miles of this gently rolling landscape, and built his impressive homestead with a commanding view over the district. A local landmark, long since deserted and ravaged by time, it is still known as the "house on Taylor's Hill".

Old Taylor house

Raglan mudflats

"Rangitahi", now used as a Bible Class camp

RAGLAN

A pleasant 48 kilometre (30 mile) drive west from Hamilton brings you to the coastal township of Raglan. From the hills around the harbour there are lovely views of the inlets and bays that stretch inland for some miles. Like other west coast beaches the landscape is rugged, and presents the artist with an interesting range of muted colours. The landscape is very different from the Waikato Basin just over the hills. At Raglan we find the rolling contours of ironsand hills, boats at rest on the tidal mudflats, weather-worn sandstone rock and dry grass.

I am a fishing man myself — anything from a sprat line on the wharf to floundering on the mudflats. With a kerosene lamp, a spear and good friends, I have spent many rewarding hours oozing stealthily along the tidal mudflats in shallow water searching for the elusive flounder. I have the usual fund of fish stories to tell, many of them originating in this harbour.

Many more Hamiltonians are discovering Raglan, and the summer months brings the town to life.

Bow Street, Raglan

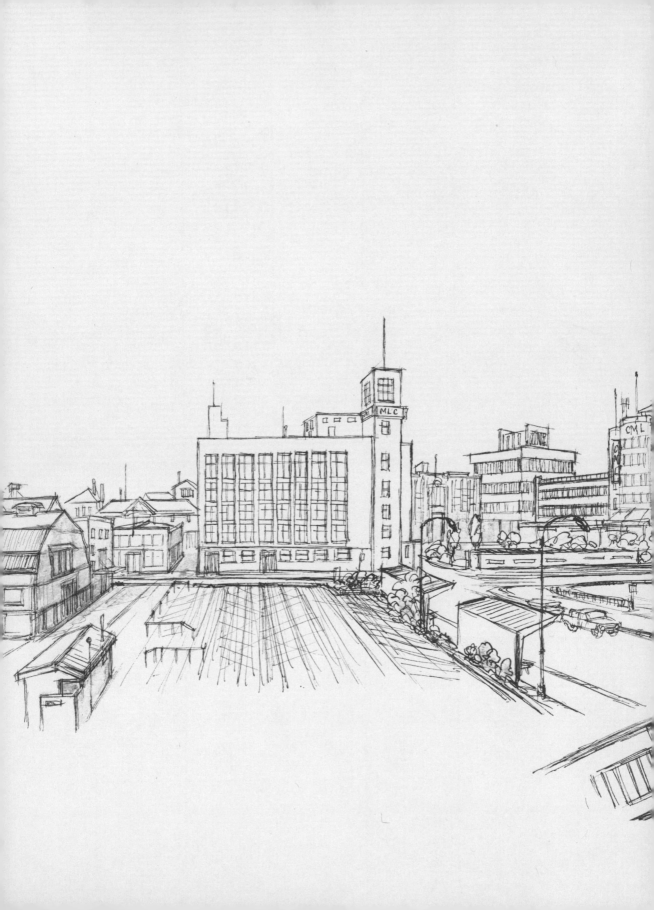